# SAY THANK YOU

# SAY THANK YOU

*poems by*
*Mikhail Aizenberg*

*translated from Russian by*
J. KATES

ZEPHYR PRESS
*Brookline, MA*

Cover art by Marco Badot
Book design by *typeslowly*
Printed by Cushing-Malloy Inc.

Several of these poems appeared previously in the following publications: *Absinthe, Crossing Centuries* (Talisman House), *Cyphers, Delos, The Dirty Goat, Glas, Green Mountains Review, Harvard Review, The Hungry Russian Winter* (n-press), *In the Grip of Strange Thoughts* (Zephyr Press), *International Quarterly, Kenyon Review, Less than a Meter* (Ugly Duckling Presse), *Modern Poetry in Translation, The Plum Review, Poetry International, River Styx, Salamander, Salt, Takahe,* and *Third Wave* (University of Michigan Press).

Zephyr Press acknowledges with gratitude the financial support of the Massachusetts Cultural Council and the National Endowment for the Arts.

NATIONAL
ENDOWMENT
FOR THE ARTS

massculturalcouncil.org

*Library of Congress Cataloging-in-Publication Data:*

Aizenberg, Mikhail.
  [Poems. English & Russian. Selections]
  Say thank you : poems / by Mikhail Aizenberg ; translated from Russian by J. Kates. -- 1st ed.
      p. cm.
  Includes bibliographical references.
  ISBN 978-0-939010-88-2 (alk. paper)
  1. Aizenberg, Mikhail--Translations into English. I. Kates, J. II. Title.
PG3478.I89A2 2007
891.71'44--dc22

                               2007003902


98765432 FIRST EDITION IN 2007

ZEPHYR PRESS
50 Kenwood Street
Brookline, MA 02446
www.zephyrpress.org

# Table of Contents

# A FIGURE OF SILENCE

> *"In its own way, verse is a unique attempt at non-literal expression: uttering a thought but avoiding the lie. The word in poetry is a figure of silence whose form is sketched out by other words. Poetry says something through movement and change. It is always existence on the edge, on the border, between illumination and inertia, between the norm and its destruction, between the life of language and simply life."[1]*

The last generation of poets that came to maturity under the regime of the Soviet Union now hears its voices echoed in English translation. Mikhail Aizenberg has lived and breathed and had his being at the heart of this generation. He has been not only one of its most eloquent practitioners, but also its chronicler and interpreter. As often happens with those who play such a role, he has spent more of his energy showcasing the work of others than his own. A reading of his thoughtful criticism and literary history is essential to any understanding of Russian poetry in the last half century, and some of his observations have achieved the notoriety of aphorism. "Without our knowing it, we live on Mars," Aizenberg wrote in "Instead of an Introduction" to a 1990 anthology of seven poets of what was then still an alternative culture, *Ponedel'nik* (Monday). And in his 1991 seminal essay that constitutes a survey of modern Russian poetry, "Nekotorye drugie" (A Few Others) he made an observation that has the air of both Moscow parochialism and magisterial perception:

> "By the mid-1970s, all poetry could be divided
> into good, bad, and 'Leningrad.' The distinction
> of the last group was that there was no way to
> tell whether it was good or bad. These poems
> seemed written not by an actual person but by a
> literary tradition."[2]

Through these wide-ranging writings, Aizenberg has consistently left out one name — his own. But if in his prose he has been the chronicler of a generation, in his poetry he has also been a significant voice in that generation — a voice that articulates the wildly erratic internal, personal climate of the political global warming that Russia has been going through. When the cultural history of Russia's turn from the twentieth to the twenty-first century is written, the epigraphs to the chapters will be drawn from Aizenberg's verses.

And so the time has come for an English-reading public to read at least a little of what his Russian colleagues and readers already know about Aizenberg's work.

Mikhail Natanovich Aizenberg was born in Moscow in 1948, and graduated from the Moscow Architectural Institute in 1972. Educated as an architect, he made restoration his specialty — a historical consciousness that shows up in his literary criticism and as very deep background in his poetry. From the beginning he immersed himself in the "underground" of Russian culture in the Soviet Union. And he made it his business to maintain and chronicle its connection with the preceding artistic and literary movements that were officially suppressed by state control.

> "Aizenberg's own apartment was the physical and intellectual locus of weekly gatherings of poets and artists, linked as much by personal ties and affections as by united cultural interests. Aizenberg's 'Mondays' — the chosen day for most of those years — embodied and continued that powerful and essential tradition of artistic interchange within circles, a tradition that has had especial importance when the political climate on the streets outside has been inclement."[3]

The movement with which Aizenberg was most closely associated during these early years has been labeled "Moscow Conceptualism," a stance that subverted the artistic canons and aspirations of the Soviet establishment by reconfiguring its own terms and exploding them from the inside. "This was the time when a series of long chains of cross-generation and cross-professional links began to emerge," the poet wrote in an account of this time. "Our associations with visual artists were the most successful: they were the most natural, and they proved the strongest over time. Many artistic works found unexpected resonance in literature."[4]

Elsewhere, he has written, "Up until the 1980s at least, poetry in Russia was not a profession but a way of life."[5] This sounds romantic to an outsider, and perhaps it was. Aizenberg has characterized those years, "In my memory, the seventies of the last century were a time of the happiest of artistic relationships."[6] But it was also a devastatingly unstable society. In September 1990, he lamented,

> "After the earlier heavy emigration of the mid-70s, when many of my closest friends left, I seemed to exist in the middle of a desert. It took many years of agonizing underground work to reconstruct a life, to build an existence. And just when it appeared that much was rebuilt, put right again, — here is the new emigration, a new hurricane, dismantling this whole fragile construction of mine."[7]

For a while he all but stopped writing verse. Yet his observational and retrospective prose blossomed, even as he despaired of ever writing poetry again. Then the times turned, the poet in Aizenberg reasserted himself. The first compilation of his poems *Ukazatel' imen* (Index of Names) was published in Moscow in 1993, followed by the chapbooks *Punktuatsiia mestnosti* (The Punctuation of Locality) in 1995 and *Za Krasnymi vorotami* (Beyond the Red Arch) in 2000; and then two more full books, *Drugie i prezhnie veshchi* (Other and Earlier Things) in that same year and, most recently, *V Metre ot nas* (A Meter Away from Us) in 2004.

For the past two decades, Aizenberg has served as a consultant to publishers and as the director of the O. G. I. poetry series, taught at the Russian State Humanitarian University (with a semester at the University of Michigan in 1994) and written a number of books of commentary on contemporary literature. In 2002, he enjoyed a Joseph Brodsky fellowship, which enabled him to travel and work in Italy, and he was awarded the Andrey Bely Prize in 2003.

The "untranslatability" of Mikhail Aizenberg's poetry lies between the lines, not in them. "Do you know what *waiting out on suitcases* means," Aizenberg's friend, Zinovy Zinik, asked me once with a kind of exasperation in his voice. "Yes," I answered, etc., etc. "But you don't know what it *means*," he insisted. It is a tone he sees as missing, an experience of life beyond the words. "His opinion of your translations," Aizenberg has written me, "is ambivalent: *They are good with reservations.* They are good because they are attuned to an American ear — with reservations because you do not always recognize the inverted clichés and other kinds of joking. But I think you know all this already."[8]

Indeed, I do know it. It's all true. There are embedded cultural and linguistic ironies and nuances that make these poems (especially the earlier ones, still vibrating with their Soviet resonances) as difficult to translate — or as impossible, if you will — as Delta blues. The most vexing example of this occurs in the poem that gives its title to this collection, where the operative word in Russian is "ксива." If ever there was a word localized in its own language and culture, this is it. As Aizenberg himself has specified:

> We have talked about "ksiva" before, you and I, but let's try again. The word itself is thieves' argot (which in Russia has always been comprehensible not just to thieves) signifying a passport or any document in general. Its etymology is problematic, but in argot, as is well known, many words are corrupted from Yiddish and Hebrew (the influence of Odessa). Just so, "ksiva" is a corruption of the Hebrew "ktuva" — "record." When I hear it, this word induces heartburn. There's something acidic ["kisloe"] about it.[9]

How do I get those layers of meaning?* I don't. I fall back on a word with its own slang connotations, but without the depth of "ксива": *ticket*. The best I can hope for is a signifier that conveys some of the irony and some of the sound of the original.

So Americans will listen to these poems with different ears from those for which they were originally written, and may well take something away from them far removed from what a Russian can. Good. Translation does not merely reiterate, it creates. For those who can read the original text, the left-hand page of a bilingual publication not only provides a corrective balance, but also liberates the right-hand page.

Aizenberg has always been very tolerant of my translations, regarding me as his collaborator rather than as his servant. It is a relationship deepened, or complicated, by a growing personal friendship over the decades. We have walked the streets of Moscow together (to walk the streets of Moscow in the company of a restoration architect is a rare treat) as well as the woods of rural New Hampshire. When we first met — two Jewish intellectuals of the same generation with similar beards, glasses and receding hairlines — I experienced the jolt of looking into an unexpected mirror. Such reflex reflection is dangerous, of course. I can fall into the trap of thinking I understand more than I do. I may take unwarranted liberties on dubious authority. For this reason, I have sought out the corrective eyes of faces that look very different from ours:

*Say Thank You* has been greatly enhanced by the editorial assistance of Matvei Yankelevich, the careful, passing eyes of Ann Komaromi, Zinovy Zinik, and the Boston translators' group I

---

*I posed the problem around a dinner-table of Russians and got a round of suggestions — "paper," "document," "ID" — none of which resolved the questions of tone.

nickname the Club Dolet. I also owe a debt of gratitude to Kent Johnson, who introduced me to the poetry of Mikhail Aizenberg on the intuition that we might make a match, and to Tatiana Shcherbina, who introduced me to the poet himself. The publication of this book has been made possible by a grant from the National Endowment for the Arts. *Say Thank You* is dedicated, of course, to Alena and Alena.

Poems in this collection, most in earlier versions, have appeared previously in:

*Absinthe, Crossing Centuries* (Talisman House), *Cyphers, Delos, The Dirty Goat, Glas, Green Mountains Review, Harvard Review, The Hungry Russian Winter* (n-press), *In the Grip of Strange Thoughts* (Zephyr Press), *International Quarterly, Kenyon Review, Less than a Meter* (Ugly Duckling Presse), *Modern Poetry in Translation, The Plum Review, Poetry International, River Styx, Salamander, Salt, Takahe,* and *Third Wave* (University of Michigan Press).

[1] Mikhail Aizenberg, "A Few Others," translated by Marian Schwartz., *Russian Studies in Literature*, vol. 32, no. 2, p. 58

[2] "A Few Others," p. 34

[3] Michael Makin, "Introduction," *Russian Studies in Literature*, vol. 32, no. 2, p. 5

[4] "A Union of Lone Wolves" (translated by Nathalie Stewart) a foreword to the anthology *In the Grip of Strange Thoughts: Russian Poetry in a New Era* (Zephyr: 1999) p. 3

[5] "A Few Others," p. 57

[6] "Минус Тринадцать по Московскому Вре," *Знамя*, Aug. 2005

[7] letter, 6 Sept. 1990

[8] letter, 9 Sept. 2005

[9] letter, 26 Nov. 2005

SAY THANK YOU

Кто из тех, кто вошел в поток,
вытянет коготок?
Ни один. Ни один не выйдет.
Ни один не вырвется невредим.

Или выйдет за всех один?

Вставшая тьмой в очах,
кто же она? —
если гибнет в тысячах,
если платит тысячей за одного сполна —

Жизнь? Повтори на слух.
Звук-то какой.
Слово само с дырой.
Или трясина сила ее порук?
Ксива — ее пароль?

Не забывай: ксива.
Не забывай, что она едва
едва выносима,
если не мертва.

И скажи спасибо

И скажи спасибо

Who of those, who of all those who stepped
into the stream will wriggle out of its grip?
Not one. No one gets out alone.
No one will get away unharmed.

Or does one only escape alone?

Rising in your eyes like darkness,
who exactly is it?
If it is to perish by the thousands
if it is to pay in full, thousands for one —

Life? Say it the way you hear it.
Quite a sound.
The word itself is riddled with holes,
the force of its guarantees a quagmire.
Is that the ticket?

Don't forget this: a ticket.
Don't forget how life is barely,
barely endurable,
if not already gone.

And say thank you

Say thank you

Что я тебе скажу
как частное лицо частному лицу —
открываешь глаза и видишь свои ладони.
Что за сон такой?
Подскажи; помоги жильцу
не поместиться в доме.

Вот он сейчас повернется к себе лицом —
где-то ему под сорок.
Что это было?
Качка, дорожный сон
в душной кабине и на плохих рессорах.

Кто это был тот, что еще вчера
в легких ходил и в добрых?
Так неопрятен вид своего добра,
что второпях бежишь от себе подобных.

Воля моя, где, — на семи ветрах
свист и высок и сладок.
Вырвется вдруг: я не червь, я не прах,
я не меченый атом в подпольных складах.

Кто разменял мне волю? Своих кругов
не узнает, ступая.
Мысль отлетает точно на пять шагов
и тычется как слепая.

I tell you this
just between us
you open your eyes and see your palms.
Is this a dream?
Hint: help the one in residence
not to make himself at home.

And now he turns to look himself in the face
somewhere just short of forty.
And this was what?
Rocking along, a traveler's dreamy sleep
in a stuffy coach on bad suspension.

Who was this who just yesterday
seemed easygoing, good-natured, too?
What's good about you is so untidy
you run away from those like you.

Where is my free will? A whistle
high and sweet on the seven winds.
Suddenly it breaks loose: I am not dust,
a worm, nor an electronic tag.

Who gave me change for my free will?
It doesn't know its own circles.
Thought flies off exactly five steps away
and stumbles, as if sightless.

Будь осторожен: нельзя попадаться навстречу
тем костылям. Не смотри на продавленный мячик.
Лучше свернуть, не ответить. И чем я отвечу
на вымогающий ужас без права подачек?

Липкая лента сбивается в яме кровати.
Ватное нёбо, как будто заложено горло,
если успеешь увидеть картуз на асфальте,
старое платье, подставку без птичьего корма.

Как неразборчиво к сердцу подсыпали крошек.
Как своевольно, как плохо она мне служила —
смертная жалость, которой я был обморожен
в детстве,
                    пока не достало тюленьего жира.

Be careful: Better not get mixed up with that fellow
on crutches. Don't look at the battered little ball.
Better to turn away. Don't answer.
What could I possibly answer
to a profitless, extortionate terror?

Cellophane won't cover a hole in the bed.
A bad taste, even a lump in your throat,
if you happen to see a cap on the pavement,
an old skirt, the perch without birdseed.

Scattered breadcrumbs on a path to the heart
With all good will, they led me nowhere —
deadly compassion, numbed by frostbite
in childhood,
            when the layer of blubber wasn't enough.

Не в печной трубе, а в газовой,
верно с первого этажа,
тихо шепчут или подсказывают,
или голосом сторожат.

Ходит гул по железной флейте —
сторожиха твердит свое,
или мысленный слабый ветер
там гуляет и так поет.

Не пугает и не забавит
голосок неизвестно чей, —
перепевы кухонных баек
и позвякиванье ключей.

Но каким-то последним звоном
все приманивает к себе,
неуверенным угомоном,
просочившимся по резьбе.

Not in the chimney, but in the gas-pipes,
coming from the first floor, for sure,
they whisper quietly, or suggestively,
or with their voices keeping watch.

A rumble runs through the iron flute —
the concierge mumbling to herself,
or a weak wind in the mind
floats singing like that one down there.

whose unknown little voice wasn't
meant to frighten or to please —
chewing over old kitchen gossip
and the jingling of keys.

But somehow with its last resonance
it keeps calling everything to itself
with an uncertain peace and quiet
percolating through the pipe-threads.

Глянь по атласу: куда
мы сегодня не уедем?
Ходит ловкая беда
как цыгане за медведем.

То до времени гурьбой,
то опять поодиночке
кто нас водит за собой
на таможенной цепочке?

И, сквозную пустоту
на цепочку запирая,
ты уходишь за черту
точно в пригороды рая.

Look through the atlas: where
shall we stay home from today?
Clever misfortune roams around
like gypsies following a trained bear.

Who is it who's taking us
linked all together in a gang
or one by one to a point in time
along the chain through customs?

But, locking a total
vacuum onto that chain,
you step outside, across the line,
as if into the suburbs of heaven.

*С. Ф.*

Это откуда? Оттуда, вестимо.
Это на фото привет от кого-то.
Это оттуда, из города Рима,
выкройки чуда —
скатерти неба, чужая столица
где-то внизу

Можно и за́ морем жить как синица, —
спать на весу,
пени платить своему долголетью
с каждого дня,

розовой медью
розовой медью
в небе звеня

*For S. F.*

Where's this one from? From there, where else.
It's a picture postcard from somebody.
It's from there, from Rome
a prodigious pattern —
celestial tablecloths, somebody else's capital
somewhere down there

maybe it's possible to live abroad like a little bird, —
to sleep in mid-air
to pay a fine for your own longevity
every day

ringing like roseate copper
roseate copper
in the sky

## ВНУТРИ КИТА

Стараюсь думать о своем,
но между прочим
я понимаю, что живьем
когда-то был проглочен.

Не надо думать: это кит.
Ну, сделай вид,
что просто заперся.
Ну, захотелось в тишине
составить из попутных записей
письмо жене:

«Одолевает духота
внутри кита».
Зачеркнуто. «Представьте, я в пещере!
А привела меня сюда
боязнь открытых помещений».

## INSIDE THE WHALE

I try to mind my own business
but somewhere along the line
it's come to my attention I've
been swallowed alive.

No need to think: this is a whale.
Look around, and, well,
as if I've locked myself in
Well, I've been wanting a bit of leisure
to organize my travel notes
into a letter to the wife:

"It's unbearably stuffy
inside a whale."
Strike that. "Imagine, the hole this place is!
What brought me here was
a fear of open spaces."

Разлинован на грядки
подмосковный лубок:
заводские початки
и фанерный грибок
у спортивной площадки,
и большой коробок
придорожной столовой —
все для ровного счета,
для печати лиловой
на книге учета.

И такой же страницей
развернулась земля,
а по ней вереницей
штемпеля, штемпеля.

Но темно и неясно,
как в хвойных лесах,
где до вечера, засветло
тень стоит на часах.

Где заметное черное?
Или белое где?
Их последние зерна
развели на воде.

Все лежит по карьерам,
по разбитым корытам
безнадежно размытым,
недостиранным, серым.

A picture of suburban Moscow
etched in garden rows:
factory-made cobs
and a plywood mushroom
at the ballpark,
and the large box
of a roadside diner —
everything for an even reckoning,
for a purple seal
in the account book

And the earth unrolled
just like the picture,
and in a line along it
stamp after stamp

But dark and undefined
as in a conifer wood
before evening, where
shadows stand on guard

Where can you see black?
And where is it white?
Their last grains floated apart
on the water

It's all lying in open diggings,
no better than at the beginning,
hopelessly washed out,
badly laundered, dirty gray.

Чтобы выйти в прямую безумную речь.
Чтобы вырваться напрямую.
Не отцеживать слово.
И не обкладывать ватой.
И не гореть синим пламенем культурной деятельности.
Нет, я не есть человек культуры.
Я — человек тоски.

О, тоска.
Единственное мое оружие.
Вечная вибрация,
от которой кирпич существования
дает долгожданную трещину

To escape into direct crazy speech.
To break out into the straightaway.
Not to strain out the word
And not to swathe it in cotton
And not burn in the blue flame of cultural activity.
No, I be no great cultural asset.
I be no man of culture.
I am a man of  profound yearning.

Ah, yearning …
My only weapon.
An everlasting vibration,
after long expectation cracking
the brick of existence.

## ПОДСТРОЧНИК

Что-то там происходит за мутным стеклом,
за преградой, запотевшей от моего дыхания.
Из подсобок и чуланов твоей жизни есть неизвестный ход
прямо на черную улицу.

Ты меня никогда не увидишь, потому что я статичен.
А тебе нужны движение и смена стоп-кадров,
ускорение и обрыв, и новая лента.
Нужны пульсации цветных огней,
бескровное зарево ночного праздника,
лихорадочное столкновение чувств.

Ради того, чтобы меня не видеть,
ты пойдешь на сделку с самой дурной сумятицей.
Но темный ее осадок ты так научилась взбалтывать,
что душа остается чистой.

# WORD-FOR-WORD

Something's happening behind the murky glass,
the other side of a barrier misted over by my breathing.
There's a little-known way out of the warehouses
            and root cellars of your life
straight into the black street.

You'll never see me because I'm not moving.
While you — you need action and stop-action,
with every new reel, acceleration and rupture.
You need the pulsation of colored lights,
the anæmic glow of a nocturnal carnival,
the feverish collision of feelings.

For the sake of keeping me invisible,
you'll strike a deal with the foulest murk.
But you've learned so well how to shake up the lees
that your soul stays clean.

Кто помнит, что за зверь «гилярная лиса»?
Была такая в жизни полоса.

В настольной книге расцелован каждый лист,
и не словами, а цитатами клялись.

Все настоящее, все выписки из книг.
Погиб поэт — отравлен ученик.

Возьми подарок. Так он жег и так саднил —
не поделиться ни с одной и ни с одним.

Цитаты кончились. Былого не вернешь.
На темный день отложен черный грош.

Свое колотится на проволке белье.
Чужое кончилось, и все вокруг свое.

Куда ни плюнь, везде свои дела.
Не хватит духу. Не хватает зла.

За поворот — и кончился обзор.
На край земли выходит робинзон.

Не всюду жизнь. Как жить? Живите так,
как вам приказывает стиснутый кулак.
Слепой прицел. Живите, изготовясь
на первый случай. На случайный знак.

Живите так, как вам подсказывает повесть.

Who now remembers what kind of animal then
a "cratic fox" was?  Those were the days, my friend.

Kisses on every page in the reference book
promises not in words, but in quotation marks.

Everything real has been excerpted from books.
The poet is slain, the reader poisoned sick.

Take what's offered. Where it touched, it burned —
it's not for handing around to just anyone.

No more quotes. You can't go home again.
A blackened penny saved for a rainy day.

Only your linen hangs snapping on the line.
Everything's over — all that you counted on.

No room to spit, your stuff all over the place.
No courage left to go on. Not enough malice.

The survey stopped where the road begins to turn.
Robinson goes to the very edge of his land.

Life has its limits. Then, how should we live?
A clenched fist shows you how. Hindsight is blind.
Live on the look-out  for the very first thing
coming along. Look for a random sign.

Live however you're prompted by the tale.

[23]

Живу, живу, а все не впрок.
Как будто время начертило
в себе обратный кувырок.
И только пыльная щетина
покрыла дни.
            Проводим год,
и время станет бородато,
как надоевший анекдот,
застрявший в памяти когда-то.

И два кочевника, два брата
ползут навстречу — кто скорей:
упрямый чукча и еврей.

Тот Ахиллес, а тот Улисс.
Один Илья, другой Микула.
Еврей и чукча обнялись.
Над ними молния сверкнула.

—

I live, I live, all to no good purpose
as if time dragged itself backwards,
topsy-turvy, as if nothing but a dusty
stubble blanketed our days.

We say goodbye to the old year
and time grows a long beard,
like a joke, hackneyed and hoary,
stuck somewhere in the memory.

There are these two nomads, brothers
creeping slowly to a rendezvous—
see who will get there first:
stubborn Chukchi or stubborn Jew.

One is Achilles, and one Ulysses.
One is Ilya, the other Mikula.
Jew and Chukchi traded kisses.
Over their heads, lightning flickered.

Нас пугают, а нам не страшно
Нас ругают, а нам не важно
Колют, а нам не больно
Гонят, а нам привольно
Что это мы за люди?
Что ж мы за перепелки?
Нам бы кричать и падать
Нам бы зубами щелкать
И в пустоте ползучей
рыться на всякий случай

They terrorize us: we are not afraid
They swear at us: but we are not dismayed
They sting us: we experience no pain
They harry us: we continue unrestrained
What kind of human beings, quailing breed
of bird are we? Weeping and weak-kneed,
What should we do but grind our teeth, creep
into the desert, and just in case, dig deep,

Этот снимок смазанный знаком:
на скамейке, с будущим в обнимку,
на скамейке поздно вечерком,
примеряя шапку-невидимку.

Незаметно, боком проберусь
по земле, где вытоптаны виды.
Вот страна, снимающая груз
будущей истории. Мы квиты.

Вся земля пустилась наутек.
Как теперь опомниться, собраться.
Помело поганое метет,
и лишай стрижет под новобранца.

Беженцы нагнали беглеца.
Все смешалось в панике обозной.
И колышет мягкие сердца
общий страх: бежать, пока не поздно.

Take this blurred snapshot for a sign:
on a bench, embracing the future,
on a bench late into the evening,
trying on the Wishing Cap.

Unnoticed, I'll sidle through a land
where everywhere you look is trashed.
Here is a country shedding the weight
of its future history. We call it quits.

The whole country took to its heels.
How to snap out of it now, buck up?
A mop scrubs at the filth and barbers
the lichen off the new recruits.

A fugitive is overtaken by the refugees.
Everything got tangled in a panicky rout.
Soft hearts are jostled by mass
fear: Run, run, before it's too late.

Свои лучшие десять лет
просидев на чужих чемоданах,
я успел написать ответ
без придаточных, не при дамах.

Десять лет пролежав на одной кровати,
провожая взглядом чужие спины,
я успел приготовить такое «хватит»,
что наверное хватит и половины.

Говорю вам: мне ничего не надо.

Позвоночник вынете — не обрушусь.

Распадаясь скажу: провались! исчезни!

Только этот людьми заселенный ужас
не подхватит меня как отец солдата,

не заставит сердцем прижаться к бездне

Having spent my ten best years
waiting on other people's suitcases
I finally wrote up an answer
without an appendix, and not for the ladies.

After ten years lying in the same bed
with my eye on the backs of exiting strangers
I cooked up my own "enough already,"
half of which was more than enough.

I'm telling you: there's nothing I need.

Extract my spine — I swear I won't cave in.

Unhinged, I say: "Collapse! Be gone!"

But the crowded horror of all this
won't catch me up like a soldier's father,

won't force my heart into the abyss

Дай живущему сил вдвойне.
В насмерть замусоренной стране
трудно жить. Ничему не равен
долгий труд выживать. Извне
только у самых глухих окраин
жить начинают, — вчерне. Но даже
в смутном сознании передовиц
днем на посту или ночью на страже,
что ни спроси, отзовется по-разному —
черным по белому,

                                белым по красному —
новое время, дыра без границ.


Тлеют каркасы. Растут штабеля.
Это открыто
как на духу отвечает земля
мертвого быта.

Let the living enjoy a double strength —
it's difficult to live in a country trashed
to death. No one is up to the drawn-out work
of surviving.
                          Only, somewhere
outside, in the farthest outskirts
they're starting to rough out a life. But even
in the dim awareness of newspapers
by day on the job or by night on guard,
you'll get different answers to any question
from the clean print of black on white,
                          from billboard white on red —
a new time, a hole without borders.

Carcasses rot. They grow in heaps.
This is clear,
how candidly the land of dead daily life
gives its answer.

Жизнь души. Душа сотрясается как листва
под дождем или — редко — под летним ветром,
задыхаясь от грозного торжества.

Представь, что ты дерево под дождем.
                           (А ведь так, наверно, и есть)
Представь, что это и есть ночная печальная правда.
Сразу многое объяснится.

Или вспомни гнездо потревоженных ос:
гулкая дрожь под пепельной оболочкой,
круговорот событий.
Сразу многое объяснится.

Многое, но не все.

Окно. Окно, открытое в сад.
Сад сияет.
Облака волокнисты или фарфоровы.

Но это не выход.

The life of the soul. The soul trembles like foliage
under the rain or in a rare summer wind,
gasping for breath in a terrifying celebration.

Imagine you are a tree out in the rain.
　　　　　(And, of course, you are.)
Imagine that this is a sad nocturnal truth.
Right away, a lot of things come clear.

Or remember the irritated hornets' nest:
a resonant tremor under its ashen shell,
the excitement of events —
Right away, a lot of things come clear.

A lot, but not everything.

A window. A window open on a garden.
The garden radiant,
clouds of filament or of porcelain.

But not a way out.

Зажигаются лампочки. Комнаты все полны
чудесами, объятьями и драками.
Хороводят мазурики новой волны
и по стенам развешивают каракули.

Это что нам показывают? Как волна
опадает, и остается тина?
Или это обрывки дурного сна
в мир выталкивает картина?

И в каком-то очерке, всех бледней,
беспокойно тянущемся к изъяну,
узнается сонная явь слепней,
прозревающих пасмурную поляну.

Lightbulbs are lit. The rooms are full
of miracles, love-making and fistfights.
The grifters of the new wave strut
and hang their fur coats along the walls.

And show us what? How the wave
ebbs, and leaves behind its slime?
Or is this the remnant of an ugly dream
a mere picture expels into the world?

In an outline, paler than any other
dragged uneasily toward the fissure
we see gadflies waking into life
and beginning to make out the misty field.

Грязное дыхание весны.
На стекле кривая полоса.
От сырой приютской белизны
клонит в сон, слипаются глаза.

Оседая, тающий намет
грудами чернеет впереди.
Остальное — черточка, пунктир,
путевого облака полет.

A dirty breath of spring.
On glass, a twisting streak.
A dry line of grayish white
induces sleep, eyelids stick.

Right before our eyes, a drift
thaws to a black mound.
What's left is a hyphen, a dotted line,
the course of a moving cloud.

А земля живет, как в последний раз.
Где она асфальт, где она атлас,
где она балласт.

Через все затейливое уныние
не заметил, желтая или синяя.
Словно зренье пустил на ветер —
не запомнил и не заметил.

Ровная линия за окном.
Вот она родина, общий дом.
Или это облако моя родина,
на глазах расходится волокном?

And the land goes on living as if at the very last
Where it's asphalt, where it's satin
where it's ballast.

And all through its flirtatious despondency
I never noticed if it was yellow or deep blue.
As if I had thrown my vision to the winds
I didn't remember and didn't notice.

An even line outside the window.
That's the motherland there, our common home.
Or is this cloud my motherland,
passing like a wisp before my eyes?

Здрасьте-здрасьте!
Битте-дритте! — пели ножницы,
Подравняем-подстрижем, какая разница!
И красиво некрасивое уложится,
серо-бурое серебряным окрасится.

Зашипит одеколон из груш оранжевых
довоенного особенного качества,
и приклеется отхваченное заживо,
или вырастет отрезанное начисто.

И легчайшее сквозное напряжение
по затылку проскользит в одно касание.
Вот исполнено твое распоряжение,
а еще какие будут указания?

Hiya-hiya! Clipper-chipper
Bitte-dritte! sang the scissors.
Snip-some, clip-some, what a difference!
Sightly with unsightly neatly fits,
steel-gray-seal-brown gets retinted silver.

Orange pears hiss toilet-water
of a special pre-war quality,
what's clipped off adheres alive
or what has been trimmed out grows right back in.

The lightest penetrating voltage
establishes contact with the skull.
Your order is effected to the letter,
what's the next command to fulfill?

Ах, это было здорово! Весело, весело.
Ах, это было невесело, — ужасно, ужасно.

Это было какое-то месиво
слухов, событий, зависти, чистоты,
нежности, зависти.
Смена страшных ночей и сказочных,
света и духоты.

И уже не тайна, что выпили чистый яд.
Господин хороший, куда ж нас теперь велят
на закон укороченный?
Господин хорунжий, товарищ уполномоченный!

Даже то, что пряталось, шло в стадах,
не всегда нелепо. Что-то почти красиво.
Неужели мы жили за просто так,
вычитаясь вон как одна рабсила?
Столько лет к дисциплине нетрудовой
привыкали ох, как мучительно,
взад-вперед в конвульсии родовой.
Холодно-горячо. Горячительно. Исключительно!

Слава тебе и хвала тебе, каждый,
что-то вписавший остатками языка.
Славен голод писчебумажный
всех, унесенных за облака,
чудом спасших себя от жажды
умереть-уснуть и не быть,

                                    не бывать пока.

Oh, it was marvelous, marvelous! what fun, what fun.
Oh, it was no fun at all! awful, awful.

It was a terrible muddle
of rumors, happenings, jealousy, innocence,
caresses, jealousy.
Nights by turns fearless and fabulous,
light and stuffiness.

Now it's no longer secret — we swallowed poison.
Good Lord, where are they sending us now
under a hurried sentence?
Good officer of the day, a comrade with power!

Even what was hidden was herded together
for some reason or other. It was almost too lovely.
And did we really live for nothing more
than to be numbered in a coffle of slaves?
For so many years, oh, we were used to
organized goldbricking, a torment
of dithering back and forth in inherited fits.
Cold-hot. Fiery hot. Really stupendous!

Glory to you and praise be to you, every one
of you who wrote something in the left-overs of language.
Glorious the hunger for something to write on
of all those, transported over the clouds,
who miraculously preserved themselves from a thirst
to die to sleep and not to exist

                              for now.

В сон затекает мелко
утренний холодок.
Белка мне снилась, белка.
А разбудил свисток.
Надо ли от озноба
вздрагивать по утрам?
Завтра увидим снова
псарню во весь экран.
Вьется тупей ретивый.
Брыла дрожат всерьез.
Свежие директивы
лает дежурный пес.

Скоро пробили сроки.
Снова остался мне
правый уклон, глубокий,
набок лицом к стене.
К суточной перебежке
и повернуться лень.

Белка моя орешки
прячет про черный день.

A morning chill leaks
little by little into my dream
of a squirrel, I dreamed of a squirrel.
I woke to a whistle's scream.
Do I need this shaking
with the morning shivers?
Tomorrow we'll see once again
a kennel projected onto every screen.
An officious jowl is quivering.
A pendulent lip trembles gravely.
The dog of the day barks
fresh directives.

Soon the final hour struck.
I was left again with a deep inclination
to lie with my face to the wall.
Sheer idleness to turn
to the daily attack.

My squirrel is storing nuts
against a rainy day.

Что я делал все время?
Я изживал свое время.
Я измышлял свою душу,
чтоб скорее, скорее
грела как батерея, —
непонятную стужу
выталкивала наружу.

Только вот что мне ни предстоит,
что там ни затевается,
стужа стоит стоит,
никуда не девается.
Так и не понял я, почему
холодно мне в ледяном дому?

А наверху Игорек-мой-свет
все что-то возится, ковыряет.
Нет, он не сводит меня на нет,
просто он времени не теряет.
Дни за днями встают рядком.
Он работает молотком.
Пилит, строгает.
Стужа его не пугает.
Всю субботу и все воскресение
он выстукивает спасение.

What was I doing all that time?
Killing time. My own.
Inventing my own soul
for it to burn, to warm me
quickly like a radiator—
to keep the unknown
killing frost at bay.

Only there's nothing for me there,
certainly not on its own account,
the deadly chill keeps on keeping on
going nowhere
And why after all should I be cold
inside a house of ice?

But upstairs my dear friend Igor
is always playing — tinkering with something.
No, he doesn't show me up,
it's just that he doesn't waste his time.
All his days proceed in order.
He works away with his hammer.
He saws, he measures, files and planes.
The frost holds no terrors for him.
All Saturday and all Sunday long
he taps out his salvation.

Это время тикает и стрекочет,
на мышиной пробуется войне.
Все, что днем ушло и забылось, к ночи
отыграет вновь на одной струне.

И как будто мне рукава зашили,
навели поддельную хрипотцу.
Лихорадка трогает сухожилья.
Паутинка бегает по лицу.

———

Now time ticks by with a nervous rattle,
battles along in a pointless war.
Everything daytime had done away with
Night plays back on a single chord.

As if someone sewed up my sleeves,
from somewhere a suspicious noise.
My tendons tremble with a fever.
A spiderweb runs along my face.

Что нам дано?
Это как сказать, что нам дано.
Угол дождя, плащевая ткань, комнатное тепло.
Кто-то сказал, что стена есть дверь.
                                        А моя стена есть окно.
И не зашторено треснувшее стекло.

Даже в него попадает последний луч,
чей-то хохот припадочный и заводной фокстрот.
Только не плачь, не плачь, умоляю тебя, не мучь.
Не говори о жизни, втиснутой между строк.

Вот подлетают голубь, ворона, грач (грач?),
чтобы отвлечь, утешить, вогнать в хандру.
Скоро покажут (только не плачь, не плачь)
облако на закате, дерево на ветру.

Как сказать: я не был причиной слез;
не восставал и не действовал заодно.
Кто-то к тебе стучался, ведь кто-то тебе принес
странную весть, что стена твоя есть окно.

—

What have we been given?
How can I say what we've been given.
An angle of rain, waterproof cloth, the warmth of a room.
Somebody said: a wall is a door.
　　　　But my wall is a window.
And the cracked glass is poorly shuttered.

Even the very last ray strikes it,
someone's spasmodic guffaw and a mechanical foxtrot.
Just don't cry, don't cry, I beg you, don't torture me.
Don't talk of a life crammed between the lines.

Here a pigeon, a crow, and a grackle (a grackle?)
all fly up to distract, to console, to drive you to the blues.
Soon we'll be given a cloud (just don't cry, don't cry)
in the sunset, a tree in the breeze.

How can I say it: I wasn't to blame for the tears;
I didn't suddenly turn up, playing that kind of game.
Somebody knocked on your door, carrying news —
a strange bit of news, that your wall is a window.

И подобно придурковатому дырмоляю
обратясь к углу шепчу ему, умоляю:
«Дыра моя, спаси меня!
Укажи дупло, где светлое спит огниво».

И к вину обращаюсь, домашнему эскулапу:
«Ты спасешь ли, излечишь меня на вечер?
Я плетню, посмотри, деревенскому стал подобен».

«Рифма! — шепчу, — видавшее виды искусство,
тяга твоя спасительна от угара.
Сколько незванных на всех твоих именинах».

Вижу луг, зеленый как до советской власти.
Корова лежит, лоснится.
«Эй, корова! — кричу, — Выручай!»

И к траве обращаюсь: «Трава,
ты всего зеленей и сильней.
Ни срубить, ни разрушить тебя невозможно,
ты начальница жизни. Спаси!»

Рифма! Дыра! Корова!
Луг и живая изгородь!
Башенка остролиста. Веточка чабреца.

Кто исцелит, кто же меня спасет?
Кто защитит от мысли, что все напрасно?

And like a silly burrowing sectarian,
turning to the corner, I whisper, begging,
"My hole, my darling, save me!
Show me the hollow where the bright tinderbox sleeps."

And I turn to wine, to that homely æsculapius:
"Will you save me, cure me when it grows dark?
Look, I've become like a wattle fence."

"Rhyme," I whisper, "you know what art is,
your pull can save me from the poison fumes.
How many just drop in on your festivities."

I see a meadow, pre-Soviet green.
A cow is lying there, gleaming and glossy.
"Hey, cow!" I shout, "Get me out of here!"

And then I turn to the grass: "Grass, you are
greener and stronger than anything alive.
Neither blight  nor mower can wipe you out —
instead, you are life's master. Save me!"

Rhyme! Hole! Cow!
Meadow and hedge!
Spire of holly. Sprig of thyme.

Who will heal, who, who will rescue me?
Who will protect me from thinking it's all useless.

А может, ты пошел назад,
как заворачивает ветер,
перебежал висячий сад,
который снизу не заметен.

В своем пространстве без углов,
растянутом прозрачной сеткой,
ты — неуемный птицелов,
ты тень, махнувшая рампеткой.

Гуляй по миру сквозняком
как посторонний и прохожий,
пока спасительный укол
рассасывается под кожей.

А что ни строчки за сто лет,
так заблудился письмоносец.
Сменить просроченный билет
готов колониальный офис.

Ложится скатертью туман.
Не охраняется граница.
Я верю: вспомнит, возвратится
любимый сын из дальних стран.

—

Just maybe you turned back
the way the wind changes direction,
ran through the hanging garden
invisible from underneath.

In your space without corners,
stretched out like a transparent web,
you are an irrepressible birdcatcher,
the shadow that waved a mothnet.

Seek your fortune like the breeze
never at home in your wandering
while an injection of salvation
reduces the itch under your skin.

What about the hundred years without a word
and the postman lost along the road.
The colonial office is now prepared
to exchange your expired ticket.

The fog floats down like a tablecloth.
No one is watching at the border.
I believe that the beloved son will remember,
and return from faraway lands.

А что действительность? Какой-то поединок?
В туманное пятно сходящий ряд картинок?
Там что-то движется (детали неясны)
как по катку скользящие фигурки.
В прожекторах зенитной белизны
зеленым вспыхивают куртки.

Или еще: хмельная пелена
и вечер, до утра катящийся мгновенно.
В холодной комнате гудящая струна,
и в легкой кофточке сирена.

—

So what is reality? A kind of single combat?
A line of pictures collecting into a cloudy blotch?
There's something moving over there (the details aren't clear)
like figures gliding on a skating rink.
In searchlights directed upward into a white sky
jackets flash green.

Or this: an intoxicated shroud, and evening
sliding in an instant all the way to morning.
In a cold room a buzzing guitar string
and a lorelei in a light sweater.

Летний закат. Золотое его тиснение
перекрывает зелень и проявляет чернь.
Все-таки многое требует объяснения.
Вот курить через силу, спрашивается, зачем?
После прогулки к озеру сердце зачем печалится?
Многое тонко спрашивается. Толком не отвечается.

Но прислонись к березе.
Но обними сосну.
Роза еще как роза. Облако тонет в озере.
По сосне
по березе ли
ножичком полосну

—

A summer sunset. Its golden imprint
exceeds the green before it goes black.
All the same, much requires explanation.
Look, why smoke more than you can?
After a stroll to the lake, what oppresses the heart?
Much is posed subtly. And not really answered.

But lean against a birch.
Embrace a pine.
A rose is still a rose. A cloud drowns in the lake.
I'll take out a penknife
and slash the pine
or the birch

Так бывает: день удачен, шаг неспешен.
Как на роликах покатится прогулка.
Друг без имени, медалями увешан,
объясняет нам названье переулка.

Друг без имени, лицо твое багрово
и военное сукно твое потерто,
напонятная замучила хвороба,
ты и вправду на ногах стоишь нетвердо.

При воскресном убывании заката
вместе с первыми движениями смуты
жизнь без повода по-своему крылата,
если светится последние минуты.

———

So it goes: a lucky day, a slow pace.
Ambling along as if on roller skates.
A nameless friend, covered with medals,
Explains the name of a little street.

Nameless friend, your face is crimson
and your military jacket is a wreck,
some unknown illness wracks you,
and you are extremely unsteady on your legs.

When Sunday's sunset fades away
along with the first indications of trouble,
life for no reason at all grows wings,
if it shines in those last few minutes.

*Д. Н.*

Это была, чтоб ты знал, политика:
взять за правило жить нигде.
Мы были письмами на воде.
И вода эта вытекла.

Вытекла, почвы не пропитав.
Это такой, чтоб ты знал, устав:
всякую речь начинать за здравие,
все оставлять на своих местах.

Что там за дверью? Никак Австралия?

*for D. N.*

This was, get it, a political matter:
make a rule to be at home nowhere.
We were like letters written on water.
And this water trickled away.

Trickled away, not soaking the earth.
This was, get it, one of the rules:
begin every speech with someone's health,
leave everything in its proper place.

And behind that door? It's not Australia?

Повернется ключ, прогремят замки,
и мои смещаются позвонки.
Мы имеем право на то, что есть.
Заоконный гул и неясный скрип
повторяет шорох моих бумаг.
Темнота умеет считать до ста.
А ночное небо, дымящий шлак,
никогда не спит, в темноте искрит,
леденит, как будто благая весть
заблудилась здесь.
И когда уходит ненужный треск,
темнота сигналит: зеро … зеро …
Повтори, что знаешь. Скажи сто раз
ничего не значащих пару фраз:

с-нами-сна-золотой-обрез
временибросовосеребро

A key turns, locks thunder
and my vertebrae shift.
We have a right to what is.
Behind the windows a vague squeaking
echoes the rustle of my papers.
Darkness knows how to count up to a hundred
but the night sky, smoking cinders, never sleeps,
sets off sparks in the darkness,
chills, as if good news got lost here.
And when the uncalled-for crackling goes away
the darkness signals: zero … zero
Repeat what you know. Say one hundred times
a couple of meaningless phrases:

"The-dream's-gold-rim-with-us"
"lowgradesilveroftime"

В этом лесу проходит граница пыли
и разложенья, заметного на границах.
Здесь собираем ягоды ли, грибы ли

Розовый свет, единый на многих лицах.
Эта земля, свернувшаяся в калачик,
как травяной, невидимый глазу улей.

Всем голосам, всем комарам — удачи!
Сколько тоски в их ненасытном гуле.

Зелень бессмертна, и существа несметны.
Тучи поющих на тысячи безголосых.
— Не унывай, — воздух стрекочет светлый, —
Я под конец объясню тебе легкий способ.

This wood is bordered by dust and rot
noticeable only at the edges.
Here we gather berries, or mushrooms.

A rosy light, the same light on many faces
This earth that has rolled up into a ball
like a grassy beehive invisible to the eye.

Good luck to every voice, to every mosquito!
Yet how melancholy is their insatiable hum.

The greenery is immortal, and the creatures numberless
Clouds of singers in thousands of the voiceless
"Cheer up," the bright air chitters,
"I'll show you an easy way nearer the end."

## 6 ЯНВАРЯ 1996

Американский лес.
Сороковой день.
Из вороненой стали сделанная луна.
Ком ледяного света. Мертвая тишина.

Воздух смыкает ставни с подлинным «никогда».
Что из руки упало, больше не откопать.
Верю: такого снега не было сотню лет.

## 6 JANUARY 1996

A forest in America.
The fortieth day.
A full moon stamped out of crow-black steel.
A lump of icy light. Dead quiet.

Air fastens the shutters with an absolute *never*.
What fell from the hands will not be unearthed.
I believe, for a hundred years there has been no snow like this.

# ЭТРУССКИЙ САРКОФАГ

*350 год до н. э.*

Темная музейная плита.
Двое рядом в каменной постели —
словно и не умерли тогда,
а, проснувшись, встать не захотели.

Под его протянутой рукой
не четвертый век до нашей эры,
а один стремительный покой,
вечный отдых с нежностью без меры.

Мягче пуха каменный ночлег
для двоих в объятье небывалом,
для любви, очнувшейся навек
под тяжелым общим покрывалом.

# AN ETRUSCAN SARCOPHAGUS

*350 BCE*

A dark slab in the museum.
Two side by side on a stone bed —
As if they were simply sleeping in,
Rather than as they are, dead.

Under his extended arm,
Forgotten, the passage of centuries,
But a certain willed, urgent calm
Eternal rest in measureless ease.

For a love that lies awake forever,
For those two in their rare embrace,
Under their heavy coverlet
A tender night softer than dust.

В этот темнеющий год
даже надежды темны.
Первая если придет
помощь — с какой стороны?

За горизонтом орда.
Хор в ожиданьи затих.
Небо, земля и вода
ждут миротворцев своих.

Тянется слой тишины
как запоздавшая весть:
с той и с другой стороны
наши сторонники есть.

Ветер впервые за нас.
И по воздушным волнам
облачный дальний запас
медленно движется к нам.

Туча меняет наклон.
Ястреб заводит крыло.
Первый лесной эшелон
в гору идет тяжело.

In this darkening year
even our hopes are dark.
If help comes, bringing first aid
it will come from where?

A horde lurks over the horizon.
A choir silent in expectation.
Heaven, earth and water
await peacemakers of their own.

A layer of quiet stretches out
like late-arriving news:
from one side and another
our allies are on the move.

The wind is in our quarter.
And along the blustery wave
obscure and far-off support
slowly comes in our direction.

A storm-cloud changes inclination.
A hawk takes wing.
The first squadron of foresters
treads heavily up the mountain.

Вдруг приходит новый,
действительно новый день —
как гигант, готовый вырубить лес.
Воздух дрожит, рассекает его клинок.
И отряд, идущий наперерез,
прочь пускается со всех ног.

В этих забавах мы еще новички.
И, как снежные хлопья выхватываются фарами,
опускается воздух, изрезанный на клочки,
рассеченный сабельными ударами.

Мельницей ходят широкие рукава.
Невредимы мельницы-исполины.
В окне появляется голова
человека, сделанного из глины.

Он непонятен вблизи, различим вдали.
Контур заметен, облик еще неясен.
Кто он — впервые вылезший из земли,
только сейчас отделивший себя от грязи?

Suddenly here comes a new,
really a brand-new day —
like a giant primed to fell a forest.
The air trembles, his blade cuts through.
And a squadron crossing our path
takes off as fast as it can.

This tormenting is still new to us.
Like snowflakes picked out by headlights,
the air falls, ripped to pieces,
split by sabre-slashes.

Wide sleeves whirl like windmills.
Unscathed windmill-giants.
At the window, the head of a man
appears, molded of clay.

Incomprehensible close up, recognizable from afar
His shape is discernible, with features still unclear.
Who is this emerging from the earth for the first time,
only just now separating himself from the muck?

—

Так проступают тайные рычаги
возле скулы и за углом щеки.
Вышли наружу силы как волдыри.
Век бы не знать, что у меня внутри.

Там недород. Битва за кислород.
Реки забиты илом. Своей тропою
звери находят мель, переходят брод,
сходятся к водопою.

Зверь в глубине
скулит по своей родне.
Птице внутри жаль своего птенца.
Волки вдвоем
в логове спят своем.
Нет у детей матери и отца.

Волк озирается: кто же тут царь зверей?
Зуд поднимает шерсть,
выставляет коготь,
чтобы узнать. Чтобы скорей, скорей
горло его достать.
Сердце его потрогать.

Secret mechanisms show through
Near the bones at the corner of the cheek
Forces erupted like blistering sores.
Never to have known what lives inside me.

A crop failure there. A battle for oxygen,
Rivers choked with silt. Wild animals
Find the bank, a ford, by their own trails,
and climb down to the waterhole.

In the depth a beast
Whimpers for its own kind,
The bird pities its fledglings,
Wolves in pairs
Sleep in their lairs,
The children have no mother or father.

A wolf looks around: who's king of beasts here?
A hunger raises his hackles,
Displays his claws
In order to know. All the more quickly
To get at its throat,
To touch its heart.

Мелкий дождик ходит тихо,
как индейский проводник.
Вот крапива, вот гречиха.
Кто садовник? Я грибник.

Елей пасмурная хвоя,
их драконья чешуя.
Но не вижу ничего я.
Ничего не слышу я.

Только слышу - тоньше вздоха
ветер ходит надо мной,
да шумит ольха-елоха
далеко за тишиной.

С неба ровно-голубого,
из недальнего угла
для живущего любого
изготовлена стрела.

Кто успеет уклониться,
лёт ее признав едва?
Вот невидимая птица
и поет как тетива.

Light rain falls as quietly
as the footfall of an Indian guide.
Nettles here, buckwheat there.
Who tends these? Not I, the mushroom-gatherer.

A cloud of spruce needles,
scales from a dragon,
but I see nothing, not I.
I hear nothing, not I.

I only hear, softer than a breath,
the wind blowing over me,
an alder-elder rustles
distantly beyond the stillness.

From the level pale blue sky
from a corner not so far away
an arrow has been fashioned
destined for anything alive.

Who will escape its barely
perceptible flight?
See how the invisible bird
sings like a bowstring.

Испугали нас нежданными салютами,
во дворе петардами. Вдвоем
ходят свет и гром ночами лютыми.
Окна открывают свет и гром.

Смерть сегодня в сахаре заварена.
Воздух с улицы идет на нас войной.
Чем отсвечивает праздничное зарево,
отвернувшись, чувствуешь спиной.

They've startled us with unexpected salvos,
with cherrybombs in the courtyard. Together
light and thunder stalk our savage nights,
light and thunder fling our windows open.

Nowadays death is brewed in sugar sacks.
Air from the street comes at us like war.
A celebratory incandescence glimmers,
you've turned away, and feel it on your back.

## ДОМАШНИЕ ГРАФФИТИ

На стене кухонной крашеной
тени праздные качаются.
Что сегодня отмечается,
никого сейчас не спрашивай.
Жизнь, похоже, намечается.

И заранее поздравь ее,
что не ищет виноватого.
Помню только фотографию,
по краям она захватана.

Вижу профили всегдашние —
теневые, но не темные —
линиями карандашными
наудачу обведенные.

Не удача нам назначена, —
только линия-обходчица,
обязательная складчина.
Но разгадывать не хочется,

теневое ли получено,
лицевое наложение?
Все равно не будет случая
повторить его движение.

## DOMESTIC GRAFFITI

On the painted kitchen wall,
idle shadows waver and sway.
This is no time to ask anyone
why today is a holiday.
Life, it seems, is moving on.

Because life isn't quick to assign blame
Congratulate it. All
I remember is a photograph
worn from too much handing around.

I see the profiles of friends —
shadowy, but not dark —
traced with pencil lines
doodled on an off-chance.

We could not count on our luck —
only the wandering outline,
a necessary pooling what we have.
But do I really want to unriddle

what we've got of the imprint
of a shadow of a face?
Never mind, it will not move
again, in any case.

У щеки проснулась слабым ветром
крохотная бабочка ночная.
Перышком летает неприметным,
чем-то о тебе напоминая.

Что-то написала, начертила, —
в зрительном движении нерезком
светопись почти неощутима
за бесцветным платиновым блеском.

Бедное трепещущее нечто.
Но в беззвучной тьме неотразима.
Только с нею тьма не бесконечна
и почти приветлива, — спасибо.

A light breeze on the cheek, no,
a tiny moth has come awake,
and flies like a negligible feather
reminding me of something about you.

It scribbled, outlined something
in a dim visual movement,
A lightscript nearly imperceptible
beyond a pallid platinum glimmer.

A pale, quivering trifle still
irresistible in the soundless darkness.
Because of it, the dark is not endless .
Indeed, nearly welcoming — thank you.

Это подземный пласт
Это другая быль
Лес для отвода глаз
Нас поцелует пыль

Радостью без причин
яростью без следа
так я себя учил
не причинять вреда

Зависть меня берет
Облачен мой недуг
Надо смотреть вперед

Мне не хватает рук
к целому возвести
век свой и опыт свой
Чтобы еще расти
надо побыть травой

This is an underground stratum
This is a different fact
Forest as a camouflage
We will be kissed by dust

Fury without consequence
joy without cause
this is what I taught myself:
Do no harm

Overwhelmed by envy
Clouded is my disease
I have to look ahead

My hands lack the strength
to bring to atonement
my own time and experience
In order to keep growing
you have to grow like grass

## КОМУ Я ЭТО ГОВОРЮ?

— Кто вы, темные, сухие, будто сложены
из шумерского бессмертного сырца?
　　　　Вы не жители, не люди вы, но кто же вы?

Или духи вы без тела, без лица?

В море мертвое, стоячее, болотное
собираются подкожные ручьи.
　　　　Тьма египетская, месиво бесплотное.

— Мы не духи. Мы не ваши. Мы ничьи.

## WHO AM I TALKING TO?

—Who are you, dark and arid as if made
out of an immortal Sumerian ore?
      You are not living things, not people, but who?

Or are you spirits, faceless, incorporeal?

Into a dead, stagnant, swampy sea
streams run together under the skin.
      An Egyptian darkness, an inchoate jumble.

— We are not spirits. We are not yours. We belong to no one.

Продолжалась жизнь без правил, спор за половину дня,
и в глазах мелькал не ужас, только слабый голод.
    Водолазка бирюзова, брюки без ремня.
    Это был не человек, а почтовый голубь.


Замечалось, что походка, хоть и шаткая, быстра.
Если кто за ним ходил, все не поспевали.
    По земле его носило легче пуха и пера,
    а исчезнет — хватятся едва ли.


Он еще высматривал, клевал свое пшено
с неуживчивой оглядкой голубиной,
    а уж было кончено; все было решено
    о его короткой жизни, страшной и невинной.

—

Life went on without rules, half of every day a quarrel,
and in his eyes glittered not terror, only a fragile hunger.
A turquoise turtleneck, trousers without a belt,
This wasn't a person, but a carrier pigeon.

It was noticed that his gait, although shaky, was quick.
Anyone following him would have trouble keeping up.
His luck carried him lightly around the land,
when he vanishes — who's to notice.

He was always on the look-out, he pecked his own millet
with an unaccommodating pigeonish caution,
but it was already all over; everything determined
in his short life, terrible and innocent.

Пилит воздух саранча
(чем Шекспир ее корит).
*Дзыга-дзыга* говорит
ветер? поворот ключа?

Вот и этот звук умолк.
Из земли выходит шелк.

Поседевший небосвод
сплошь булавками исколот.
Неба пропасть, переход
в невесомый ртутный холод.

A cicada saws the air thus
(Shakespeare reproaches it for that).
What is saying *djiga-djiga* —
the wind? The turn of a key?

Suddenly there is no sound.
Silk emerges from the ground.

The firmament has turned gray
pricked all over with pins.
The abyss of heaven, a passageway
Into weightless quicksilver cold.

Есть в них что-то от пустого
и бессолнечного дня:
не прохладная истома,
не оттенок ячменя,
но глаза нетерпеливо
не темнеют никогда.
Нет внезапного прилива,
ни опасного отлива,
нет русалочьего льда.
Чем затянешь во стремнину,
в пагубную глубину?
Там речную прячешь глину,
я на глину не взгляну.

They have in them something
from the empty and sunless day:
Not a chilly languor,
Not a tint of golden wheat,
But these eyes never
Darken with impatience.
Is there no sudden flood,
No dangerous ebb,
Is there no siren ice,
To draw you into the rapids,
Into the baneful depth?
Down there you are hiding the river clay,
I will not look at the clay.

Это лицо тайное вычитанье
переживает каждой своей чертой.
В нем проступает твердое очертанье,
угол какой-то — пятый или шестой.

Для голосов смутных или тревожных
виден предел: дальше им хода нет.
Лобная кость, мыслей ее заложник,
костная ткань знает прямой ответ.

This face endures a secret subtraction
from each of its lines.
the hard outline shows through it,
some corner or other — the fifth or sixth.

There is an obvious limit to disturbed
or uneasy voices: there is no road past them.
The frontal bone, hostage to its thought,
the fabric of bone knows a direct answer.

Дети, где вы?
Дети где-то в шалаше.
Дети по звериным тропам
путешествуют автостопом.

Может, недалеко уже.

Мы дикари. Ноги у нас пятнисты.
Рожи черны.
Дети выросли вместе с нами,
но не во все еще посвящены.
Лица просты их, глаза травянисты.
Странны им наших законов полотнища
с полупонятными именами.

Хоть бы не встретился кто-то из нас
им на дороге.
Лучше со стадом король-свинопас.
Лучше вороны, стрижи и сороки.
Ящерица на припеке.

Children, where are you?
The children are out somewhere camping,
The children are hitchhiking
along trails made by animals.

Maybe not that far away.

We're wild men. Our legs are dappled.
Our snouts black.
The children have grown up among us,
but not yet been fully initiated.
Their faces are simple, their eyes insipid.
Strange to them the tablets of our laws
with half-understood names

If only one of us hadn't met them
Along the road.
Better a swineherd-king with his pigs.
Better magpies, martins, and crows.
A lizard in the sun.

Там еще с ночи тянуло дымком.

Дружный такой оказался поселок:
ведра прикованы
шланги бракованы
краны прикручены

Главное, всюду вода под замком.

Пусто. А ветер попутный как раз
гонит огонь от дымящихся елок.
Желтый за сереньким прячется дымом —
это и есть отравляющий газ,
как ты уйдешь от него невредимым.

Чисто сработано.
Пекло-то вот оно —
в метре от нас.

All night, smoke hung in the air.

The suburb seemed so genial:
buckets on chains
hoses defective
faucets turned off

All the water under lock and key.

Empty. But suddenly a fair wind
chases the fire away from smouldering spruce.
A yellow fog hides behind a grayish smoke —
it's really a poisonous gas,
you can't get away from it unharmed.

A group effort.
That's the hellish heat —
a meter away from us.

Давным-давно один еврей
здесь жил. (А нам какое дело?)

Чужая шуба, у дверей
висящая, полуистлела.

Нет коммунального угла.
Своя у каждого жилплощадь.

Но шуба все еще цела,
и в темноте страшна на ощупь.

Once upon a time a certain Jew
Lived here (what's that to me and you?)

Somebody left, behind the door,
A mangy fur coat, hanging there.

This is not a communal flat,
Each of us has his personal spot.

But that fur coat is safe and sound,
And in the dark is terrible to the touch.

Птицы молчат.
Плотная тень на придымленной чаще.
День, омраченный сходом неравных сил.
Тьма наступает, ее холодящий чад.
Облачный край и отсвет его щадящий.
Мне ли не знать: ни разу не пощадил.

The birds are silent.
A heavy shadow in a smoke-obscured thicket.
The day, overmastered by a gloomy nightfall.
Darkness advances, with an intoxicating chill.
Reflected twilight lingers at the edge of a cloud.
Who could know better than I: it has never given comfort.

# NOTES

(those in italics, the author's own)

**p. 3: ticket:** See the introduction.

**p. 23:** *"cratic fox"was a misprint in the first Russian edition of* Nabokov's Lolita: *"cratic" instead of "arctic." The whole poem is an address to a small circle, a brotherhood of readers of this first edition — only they can know what a "cratic" fox is, because there's no such word.*

**p. 25: Chukchi, Jew:** The Siberian Chukchi and the eastern European Jew stand not only at opposite geographic ends of the Russian expanse; but the Chukchi is proverbial for simplicity and the Jew for craftiness. Ilya (Muromets) and Mikula (Selianinovich) are heroes of medieval Russian folk poetry.

**p. 55: burrowing sectarian:** The Russian word refers to a particular sect of troglodyte Christians.

**p. 71: The fortieth day** after a person's death is, in Russian tradition, a formal marker of mourning.

**p. 83: sugar sacks** as used by terrorists to pack explosives.

**p. 93:** *This poem is about the death of the poet Anatoly Makovsky, who disappeared without a trace a few years ago, obviously murdered. He loved to go from city to city, just wander around, he was practically homeless. His friends wouldn't worry if they had no news of him.*

**p. 95**: *Hamlet* III.2.

**p. 105**: *This poem is set in a very specific place in Moscow: next to the "salt cellars," that is, on the Solyanka. Here (in Starosadsky Lane) Mandelstam lived in the early 1930s — in his brother's room in a communal apartment. It was here that he wrote his well known poem "Aleksandr Gertsevich, the Jewish musician," in which there is the line: "To hang there like a black fur coat on a coat-rack." This is the same fur coat hanging from that time until now in that apartment where O. M. once lived. I don't know how to reflect this in the translation. I don't know who among Russian writers understands this music. But it's important to me that you know it.*